George Orwell

Animal Farm

Text adaptation and activities by **Gina D.B. Clemen**
Illustrated by **Franco Rivolli**

© 2022 D Scuola SpA
Via Privata Mondadori, 1 – 20054 Segrate (MI)
First edition: February 2022

We would be happy to give you further information concerning our material and receive your comments.
info@blackcat-cideb.com
blackcat-cideb.com

Content editor: Maria Grazia Donati
Editor: Massimo Sottini
Design: Erika Barabino, Silvia Bassi, Daniele Pagliari
Page Layout: Annalisa Possenti
Picture research: Alice Graziotin
Art Director: Carla Nadia Maestri

DEALINK, DEAFLIX are trademarks licensed by De Agostini SpA

Picture credits:
Adobe Stock; Shutterstock; iStockPhoto; Pictures from History / Bridgeman Images:4; Batchelor, Joy and Halas, John / Bridgeman Images: 5; Ben Birchall / PA Images via Getty Images: 31; Universal History Archive / UIG / Bridgeman Images: 90; Sovfoto / UIG / Bridgeman Images: 92.

All rights reserved. No part of this book may be reproduced, stored in a retrieval system or transmitted, in any form of by any means, electronic, mechanical, photocopying, recording or otherwise, without the written permission of the publisher.

Member of CISQ Federation

CERTIFIED MANAGEMENT SYSTEM
ISO 9001

The design, production and distribution of educational materials for the CIDEB (Black Cat) brand are managed in compliance with the rules of Quality Management System which fulfils the requirements of the standard ISO 9001

Reprints
10   9   8   7   6   5   4   3   2   1
2031   2030   2029   2028   2027   2025

Printed in Italy by Litoprint srl – Genoa

Contents

CHAPTER 1	*Old Major*		8
CHAPTER 2	*The Rebellion*		16
CHAPTER 3	*The Seven Commandments*		24
CHAPTER 4	*Nine new puppies*		33
CHAPTER 5	*Battle of the Cowshed*		41
CHAPTER 6	*A surprising announcement*		50
CHAPTER 7	*The November storm*		59
CHAPTER 8	*The banknotes*		67
CHAPTER 9	*Explosives!*		76
CHAPTER 10	*Boxer*		82

DOSSIERS	George Orwell	4
	Animal Farm: An Allegory	90

ACTIVITIES	Before you read	7, 15, 23, 40, 49, 58, 75
	The text and beyond	13, 21, 29, 38, 47, 56, 65, 73, 80, 88
	After reading	94

B1 PRELIMINARY   This icon indicates Preliminary-style activities

T: GRADE 5   This icon indicates Trinity-style activities

   THE STORY IS FULLY RECORDED.

George Orwell

Eric Arthur Blair's pen-name was George Orwell. He was born in Motihari, India, on 25 June 1903. His parents were British and his father worked for the British Government in India.

When Orwell was a young child, his mother took him to England to have him educated there. He went to St Cyprian's Preparatory School, and then to Eton College.

In 1922 Orwell joined the Indian Imperial Police in Burma (now called Myanmar), a British colony. He found the job was boring so, in 1927, he returned to England and decided to become a writer. In 1928 he moved to Paris and he did several different jobs. This was a very difficult time for Orwell, and as he was poor he often didn't have enough to eat. He wrote about his experiences in an autobiographical book called *Down and out in Paris and London* (1933). He published his first novel, *Burmese Days*, in 1934.

Late in 1936, during the Spanish Civil War, Orwell travelled to Spain to fight for the Republic, against Franco's Nationalists. However, he had to escape from Spain because of serious political problems. Orwell's novel *Homage to Catalonia* (1938) was inspired by his experiences in Spain.

In 1943 Orwell became the literary editor of *The Tribune*, a weekly magazine. By now he was a well-known journalist in Great Britain.

Orwell was very much against dictators [1] and Stalin's Revolution in

---

1. **dictator**: a person who has complete power in a country.

Russia (1928-1953). So, in 1945 he decided to write a satire [2] on Stalinism in a fable [3] called *Animal Farm*, and it became a very successful work. In 1948 he wrote *Nineteen Eighty-Four*, a frightening novel about a totalitarian [4] society of the future. It was a bestseller all over the world.

The adjective 'Orwellian' has become a part of everyday language, because it describes social and political systems that can destroy a free and open society.

Orwell's poor health led to his death on 21 January 1950. He was buried at the Church of all Saints in Oxfordshire, England.

Comprehension check

1 Answer the following questions.

1. Why were George Orwell's parents living in India?
2. Why did Orwell's mother take him to England?
3. Which schools did Orwell attend?
4. Why did Orwell go to Burma?
5. What was Orwell's life like in Paris?
6. Why did Orwell go to Spain?
7. Why did Orwell decide to write *Animal Farm*?
8. What was *Nineteen Eighty-Four* about?

---

2. **satire** : use of humour or exaggeration to show how foolish some people's behaviour or ideas are.
3. **fable** : a story that teaches a moral lesson; animals are often the main characters.
4. **totalitarian** : political system where there is only one political party that controls everything and does not allow opposition parties.

ACTIVITIES

Before you read

Vocabulary

1 Match the words with their meanings. Use a dictionary if necessary.

1 ☐ pop-holes   3 ☐ rebellion   5 ☐ gallon
2 ☐ to slaughter   4 ☐ foal   6 ☐ mare

a A violent organized action by a large group of people who want to change a social system.
b A very young horse.
c Unit of measurement for liquids; equal to about 4 litres.
d To kill animals to sell their meat.
e A female horse.
f Little holes where hens can enter and exit the barn.

Vocabulary

2 Match the words with the correct picture. Use a dictionary if necessary.

1 ☐ barn   3 ☐ cart   5 ☐ trotter
2 ☐ straw   4 ☐ raven   6 ☐ plough

Speaking

3 Look at the characters on page 6. Which animals do you think will be the protagonists of the story and why?

CHAPTER **1**

OLD MAJOR

Mr Jones was the owner of Manor Farm. At night he always locked the hen-houses, but he was too drunk to remember to shut the pop-holes. He slowly walked across the yard, left his boots outside the back door and drank a last glass of beer. Then he went to bed and Mrs Jones was already asleep.

As soon as the light in the bedroom was off, there was excitement and noise in the farm buildings.

Old Major was the prize-winning[1] boar, or male pig, of Manor Farm. He was twelve years old and quite handsome for his age. All the farm animals respected him because he was very wise. One night, Old Major had a strange dream and, the next day, he wanted to tell the other animals about it.

---

1. **prize-winning** : this boar won many prizes at farm fairs.

OLD MAJOR

The word got around and all the farm animals went to the big barn to listen to him. There was a small platform and Old Major was already comfortably seated there.

The first ones to arrive were the three dogs, Bluebell, Jessie and Pincher. Then the pigs came and sat on the straw in front of the platform. The hens and the pigeons were near the windows and the sheep and the cows lay down behind the pigs. Clover and Boxer were two big horses and they came in together, walking slowly. Clover was a mare and mother of four foals. Boxer was an enormous horse; he was stronger than two ordinary horses! He wasn't very intelligent, but the animals liked and respected him because he was a great worker.

After the horses, Muriel and Benjamin arrived. Muriel was a white goat and Benjamin was a donkey. He was the oldest animal on the farm, and he also had a bad temper.[2] He rarely talked and he never laughed because he said there was nothing to laugh about. However, on Sundays he usually stayed with Boxer on the grassy field.

At the last moment, Mollie, the silly white mare arrived. She pulled Mr Jones's cart and she felt very pretty and important. The cat was the last one to get there and he chose the warmest place to sit — between Boxer and Clover. He didn't listen to what Old Major was saying. The old raven Moses was not present.

'Comrades,'[3] said Old Major, looking kindly at the animals, 'I don't think I'll be here much longer, but before I die, I want to tell you some very important things. I've had a long life and I've seen many things. I understand the world of us animals.' He stopped for a moment and then continued. 'Our lives are miserable and short! We are born and we are given just enough food to keep us alive.' 'We must work hard,

---

2. **bad temper**: when you get angry quickly.
3. **comrade**: a friend, especially one that you shared a difficult situation with.

CHAPTER 1

very hard, and when we are no longer useful, we are slaughtered with terrible cruelty. No animal in England knows the meaning of happiness. No animal in England is free. We are all slaves, and that is the truth!' All the animals were listening carefully, except for the cat. 'But why are we in this condition?' Old Major continued. 'Because nearly all the product of our work is stolen from us by human beings! Our big problem is: Man. Man is the only real enemy we have. Man is the reason why we are always hungry and we work too much.'

The animals looked at each other amazed.

'Comrades, Man is the only creature who eats and drinks without producing anything. He doesn't give milk, he doesn't lay eggs and he's too weak to pull the plough. But he's the master of all the animals! Is that right?' cried Old Major, angrily. 'You cows have given thousands of gallons of milk this year, and they have all been sold to make money for Mr Jones. And you hens, how many eggs have you laid this year? And how many of those eggs have become young chickens? Very, very few!' The hens looked at each other, confused.

Old Major looked at Clover and said, 'Clover, you are the proud mother of four foals, but each foal was sold at the age of one year. You'll never see your foals again!' Clover looked at Boxer with sad eyes and shook her head slowly.

Old Major raised his voice and said, 'And last of all, no animal escapes the cruel knife at the end! Oh, what horror! We are sent to the slaughterhouse when we are no longer useful! And when dogs become old and useless, Jones ties a stone around their necks and drowns them in the lake!' Sounds of complaint were heard in the big barn.

'Comrades, listen!' cried Old Major, raising his trotter. 'If we get rid of Man, the product of our work will be our own! And we will become rich and free! My message to you is Rebellion! I don't know when the Rebellion will come, but sooner or later it will happen!'

CHAPTER 1

'And remember, never listen when they tell you that Man and animals have a common interest. It is a big lie! Man's only interest is himself! Whatever goes on two legs is an enemy. Whatever goes on four legs, or has wings, is a friend. All animals are brothers and all animals are equal.'

At this moment all the animals cried out in agreement and there was great excitement in the big barn.

'Now, comrades,' said Old Major, 'I will tell you about my dream last night. When I was a little pig my mother and the other pigs sang an old song. Last night it came back to me in my dream. It's called "Beasts of England". My voice is old and not very musical, but I'll sing it to you:'

Beasts of England, beasts of Ireland,
Beasts of every land,
Listen to this message!
Soon or late the day will come
We will rebel against our enemy, MAN!
And we will win!
Then we will all be free and happy,
Forever and ever!

The song created the wildest excitement and soon all the animals were singing it by themselves. The clever ones, like the pigs and the dogs, learned the words of the entire song immediately. Even the stupid ones quickly learned the tune. Unfortunately, the loud noise that came from the barn woke up Mr Jones. He thought there was a fox in the yard and got his gun. He started to shoot in the darkness and the meeting in the barn ended immediately. All the animals quickly went back to their own sleeping places and the whole farm was silent.

The text and *beyond*

Comprehension check

1 Read the sentences about Chapter 1 and decide if each sentence is correct or incorrect. If it is correct, put a tick (✔) in the box under A for YES. If it is not correct, put a tick (✔) in the box under B for NO.

		A	B
1	Mr Jones didn't shut the pop-holes and all the hens escaped.	☐	☐
2	Old Major was a prize-winning boar.	☐	☐
3	Old Major wanted to tell the animals about a dream he had.	☐	☐
4	Clover and Boxer didn't listen to what Old Major was saying.	☐	☐
5	The worst tempered animal on the farm was Muriel.	☐	☐
6	Mr Jones's cart was pulled by Mollie.	☐	☐
7	Old Major said that the lives of the animals were short and miserable.	☐	☐
8	When animals were no longer useful, Mr Jones sold them to another farmer.	☐	☐
9	As Man was the enemy of the animals, Old Major hoped for a rebellion.	☐	☐
10	None of the animals learned the new song because the words were too difficult.	☐	☐

Grammar: nouns and adjectives

2 **A** Fill in the table with the missing noun or adjective.

NOUN	ADJECTIVE
comfort	1 ....
2	cruel
hunger	3 ....
4	free
confusion	5 ....
6	excited
sadness	7 ....
8	noisy

B Now write four sentences about the story using nouns and adjectives in the table.

Time clauses

As soon as the light in the bedroom was off, there was excitement and noise in the farm buildings.
We are sent to the slaughterhouse **when** we are no longer useful.
Time clauses show when something happens. They are introduced by conjunctions.
Mr Jones went home **after** he shut the hen-houses.
Everyone was silent **when** Old Major came into the barn.
'I'll wait for you **until** three o'clock,' said the young girl.
Mr Jones read the newspaper **while** Mrs Jones was having breakfast.

Grammar: time clauses

3 Complete the sentences with the words from the box.

> until   when   before (x2)   after   while   as soon as

0   The new barn won't be ready ……… until ……… next year.
1   All the animals listened ……………… Old Major was talking.
2   The farmers were tired and went home ……………… a long day at work.
3   The children washed their hands ……………… eating their lunch.
4   The animals ran to the barn ……………… it started raining.
5   Mr Jones got angry ……………… he heard the loud noise in the barn.
6   The children were always hungry ……………… dinner.

Reading pictures

4 Look at the picture on page 11 and answer these questions.

1   Where are the animals?
2   Who is the center of attention and why?
3   Which animals are present?

ACTIVITIES

Before you read

Vocabulary

1 Match the words with the correct picture.

1 horn
2 whip
3 ribbon
4 chain
5 corn

2 Match the words with their meanings. Use a dictionary if necessary.

1 ☐ hay
2 ☐ to butt
3 ☐ storage shed
4 ☐ tough
5 ☐ to stare
6 ☐ to bury

a A small building on a farm where the farmer keeps food for the animals.
b To look at for a long time.
c Grass that was cut and dried, and is then used to feed horses and other animals.
d To hit hard with the top of the head.
e To put something under the ground.
f Determined, not easy to deal with.

15

CHAPTER **2**

THE REBELLION

Three nights later, Old Major died peacefully in his sleep. His body was buried in the garden. This happened early in March and during the next three months there was a lot of secret activity on the farm. The animals didn't know when the rebellion could take place, but they wanted to prepare for it.

As the pigs were the smartest animals, they had the job of teaching and organizing the others. Two young boars named Napoleon and Snowball were the leaders. Napoleon was a large, tough boar with a strong character. He didn't talk a lot and he usually did everything he wanted to do. Snowball was livelier than Napoleon and he was a big talker.

There were several other young pigs on the farm. Squealer was a small fat pig with round cheeks, bright eyes and a high voice. He was a brilliant talker and was always able to convince others.

THE REBELLION

The three of them created the principles of Animalism, a complete set of ideas from Old Major's teachings.

Several nights a week, when Mr Jones was asleep, Napoleon, Snowball and Squealer held secret meetings in the big barn. They wanted to teach the principles of Animalism to the others, but it wasn't easy. They found that some of the animals were quite stupid.

'Mr Jones is our Master,' said one of the older sheep. 'If he goes away, who will feed us?'

'Who cares what happens on the farm after we're dead?' asked a cow.

Mollie, the white mare, asked the silliest question, 'Will there still be sugar after the Rebellion?'

'No,' said Snowball firmly. 'We can't make sugar on this farm. Besides, you don't need sugar. You'll have lots of sweet grass.'

'And can I still wear ribbons on my pretty head?' asked Mollie.

'Comrade,' said Snowball, 'those ribbons show that you are a slave of Mr Jones! Don't you understand that freedom is more important than ribbons?'

Mollie agreed, but she was not convinced.

Napoleon, Snowball and Squealer had a very hard time with Moses, the raven. He was Mr Jones's special pet and also his spy. He never did any work, but he was very clever. He liked telling the animals all kinds of lies that some of them believed.

One day Moses was talking to the animals and said, 'Did you know that when animals die they go to Sugarcandy Mountain, a beautiful place above the clouds?'

The answer from most of the animals was, 'Oh... really! We didn't know!' They stared at him with their hopeful eyes.

Moses continued, 'On Sugarcandy Mountain it's Sunday every day of the week, and there's plenty of sweet grass and sugar!'

CHAPTER 2

The pigs were angry and Napoleon said, 'What nonsense!¹ Don't listen to Moses and his lies! Get out of here, Moses!'

The two horses, Boxer and Clover, were simple creatures. They certainly didn't do much thinking, but they listened to everything the pigs said. They considered the pigs their teachers and passed on the information to the other animals. Boxer and Clover never missed a secret meeting in the barn and they led the singing of 'Beasts of England'.

Mr Jones was a good farmer, but recently he had money problems. He stopped working on the farm and started to drink. He was often drunk and forgot to feed the animals. The men who worked for him were lazy and dishonest, and the farm was in poor condition. No one cut the grass in the month of June. Mr Jones spent more and more time drinking beer at the Red Lion Pub. And no one remembered to feed the poor animals who were terribly hungry.

One of the hungry cows broke the door of the storage shed with her horns. All the other animals ran to the shed and started to eat the corn and the hay. The noise woke up Mr Jones who was sleeping on a chair in the kitchen.

'What... what's happening?' he asked, looking at the animals at the storage shed. He called his four helpers and cried, 'Get the whips! Stop those animals! Whip them! Whip them hard!'

The animals didn't plan a rebellion, but they were very hungry and very angry. The whips hurt them and they rebelled for the first time in their lives! These strong animals kicked and butted Mr Jones and his men.

'These animals have gone crazy!' cried Mr Jones, running away. 'I've never seen anything like this! Let's get out of here!'

---

1. **nonsense** : something foolish or stupid.

CHAPTER 2

The furious animals chased the five frightened men down the road and shut the big gate in their faces. From the bedroom window, Mrs Jones saw what was happening. It was a frightening scene! She quickly put a few things in a big bag and ran away from the farm. For the first few minutes the animals couldn't believe their luck.

But the animals hadn't finished yet. They proudly galloped around the farm to make sure that no man was hiding there, and then they went back to the farm buildings. They built a fire and threw the whips, the knives, the chains and all the other things that were part of Mr Jones's world into the big fire. The animals destroyed everything that reminded[2] them of Mr Jones. That evening all the animals sang 'Beasts of England' seven times and then slept a long, peaceful sleep.

The next morning the animals woke up at dawn as usual, and they remembered the wonderful victory of the day before. They ran out into the field and up to a small hill. From the hill they had a beautiful view of the farm, and it was theirs! They were extremely happy, and ran around and played in the green grass.

Then the animals went to the Jones farmhouse. It was theirs, too, but they were afraid to go inside. Snowball and Napoleon pushed the front door open and the animals entered slowly and quietly. They didn't want to break anything. They stared at the unbelievable luxury of the things around them: the comfortable sofa, the big, soft bed, the lovely carpet, the picture of Queen Victoria on the wall. All of these luxuries belonged to Man!

Napoleon looked at the animals and announced, 'This farmhouse will be a museum, and no animal must ever live there!' Everyone agreed with Napoleon.

---

2. **reminded** : made them remember.

ACTIVITIES

The text and *beyond*

Comprehension check

1 **Answer the following questions.**

1. What was the job of the pigs and why?
2. Who was tough and had a strong character?
3. What were the principles of Animalism?
4. What was Mollie worried about?
5. What did Moses the raven tell the animals?
6. Why was Mr Jones's farm in poor condition?
7. What did one of the hungry cows do?
8. How did the animal rebellion end?
9. Why did the animals build a big fire?
10. What did the animals see inside the Jones's farmhouse?

Sentence transformation

2 **For each question, complete the second sentence so that it means the same as the first. Use no more than three words.**

0. It wasn't easy to teach the animals the new song.
   It was ....*difficult*........ to teach the animals the new song.
1. The storage shed wasn't far from the farmhouse.
   The storage shed .... the farmhouse.
2. Clover was not as big as Boxer.
   Clover was .... Boxer.
3. The animals preferred summer weather to winter weather.
   The animals liked summer weather .... winter weather.
4. No one liked Benjamin the donkey.
   Benjamin the donkey was ....
5. There was nobody in the farmhouse.
   There wasn't .... the farmhouse.

Yet

*But the animals hadn't finished **yet**.*
We use ***yet*** with negative statements in the present perfect to show that something has not happened, but it could happen later.
*She hasn't been to the bookshop **yet**.   They haven't tasted the cake **yet**.*
We also use ***yet*** with questions in the present perfect to ask if something has happened, usually something we're expecting to happen.
*Has he talked to the teacher **yet**?   Have you found the keys **yet**?*

Grammar: *yet*

3 Reorder the questions and match them with the answers.

1. ☐ you / fed / yet / the animals / Have / ?
2. ☐ she / Mrs Jones / yet / Has / talked to / ?
3. ☐ barn / they / the / yet / Have / cleaned / ?
4. ☐ the sugar / Has / bought / he / yet / ?
5. ☐ yet / you / Have / read / my letter / ?
6. ☐ he / seen / yet / Has / the new horse / ?

a Yes, she talked to her this morning.
b No, he hasn't seen it yet.
c No, I haven't fed them yet.
d Yes, they cleaned it yesterday.
e No, he hasn't bought it yet.
f Yes, I read it a few minutes ago.

T: GRADE 5

Speaking: means of transport

4 Mr Jones uses a horse and a cart as a means of transport. Today there are several different means of transport. Talk with your partner about means of transport. Use these questions to help you.

1. What means of transport do you prefer and why?
2. Which means of transport is most and least polluting?

ACTIVITIES

Before you read

Listening

1 Listen to Chapter 3 and choose the correct answer — a, b or c.

1 Where did Snowball write the Seven Commandments?

A B C

2 Which animal never did any work?

A B C

3 Who was a real work champion?

A B C

4 What colour was the Animal Farm flag?

A B C

CHAPTER **3**

THE SEVEN COMMANDMENTS

fter leaving the farmhouse Snowball said, 'Comrades, we have a long day ahead of us. Today we're going to cut the grass, so that we'll have lots of hay for the winter. But first there's something important I must tell you. During the past three months Napoleon, Squealer and I have learned to read and write! We found an old spelling book that belonged to Mr Jones's children and we taught ourselves many things.'

There was a general sound of surprise from the other animals: 'AH... UH... OH...'

Napoleon suddenly appeared with two buckets[1] of black and white paint, and he led the way to the big gate on the main road.

---

1. **bucket** :

THE SEVEN COMMANDMENTS

Snowball took a brush with his trotter and erased the name MANOR FARM from the sign. In its place he painted the words ANIMAL FARM, in big letters. This was the new name of the farm and the animals looked at it in amazement.

'Now follow me to the barn!' cried Napoleon, excitedly.

When all the animals got to the barn Napoleon and Snowball spoke to them. Napoleon said, 'During the past three months we pigs have studied the principles of Animalism and it was hard work! We have decided on the Seven Commandments that Snowball is going to write on the barn wall.'

Squealer held the tall ladder and Snowball climbed up carefully because it wasn't easy for a pig to climb up a ladder. Squealer held the heavy bucket of paint and Snowball started to write. He wrote the Seven Commandments in huge white letters so that everyone could read easily.

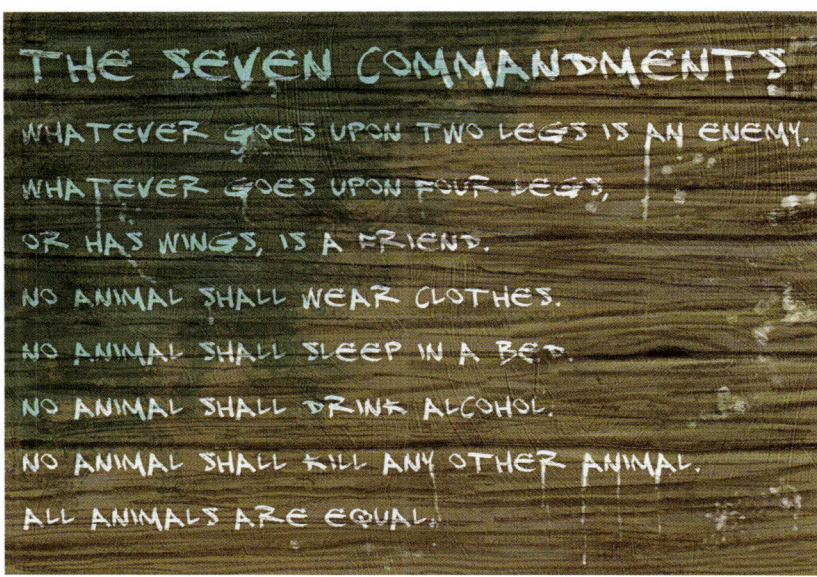

THE SEVEN COMMANDMENTS
WHATEVER GOES UPON TWO LEGS IS AN ENEMY.
WHATEVER GOES UPON FOUR LEGS,
OR HAS WINGS, IS A FRIEND.
NO ANIMAL SHALL WEAR CLOTHES.
NO ANIMAL SHALL SLEEP IN A BED.
NO ANIMAL SHALL DRINK ALCOHOL.
NO ANIMAL SHALL KILL ANY OTHER ANIMAL.
ALL ANIMALS ARE EQUAL.

Chapter 3

Then Snowball read the seven commandments aloud for everyone to hear and understand. All the animals agreed and the smarter ones learned the commandments by heart.[2]

'Now, comrades, let's get to work!' said Snowball. 'We must cut the hay faster than Jones and his men did!'

At that moment three of the cows were complaining because no one milked them. The pigs got the buckets and milked the cows successfully. Soon there were five buckets of creamy milk and the animals looked at them with interest.

'What's going to happen to that good milk?' asked one of the sheep.

'Jones always mixed lots of it in our feed,' said one of the hens.

'Don't worry about the milk, comrades!' said Napoleon, standing in front of the five buckets. 'The hay is more important now. Comrade Snowball will lead the way and I will follow in a few minutes! The hay is waiting for us!'

So the animals followed Snowball to the field and began to work. When they returned in the evening the milk wasn't there anymore.

The animals worked hard during the harvest.[3] Sometimes it was difficult to use certain tools[4] as these tools were made for humans, and not for animals. Boxer and Clover worked especially hard, never stopping to rest. The harvest was successful and bigger than the years before. The pigs didn't work because they directed and supervised the others. With their superior knowledge it was natural that they were the leaders.

All through the summer the work on the farm went smoothly. The animals were happy, and they were never hungry or very tired. There were no fights and nobody stole anything.

---

2. **by heart**: from memory, when you remember something without reading it.
3. **harvest**: when you gather the crops in the fields; the vegetables, the fruit.
4. **tool**: a piece of equipment that helps you do certain work, like a hammer.

CHAPTER 3

Everyone worked hard except for the cat. She often disappeared for hours when there was work to be done. However, when she returned she always had excellent excuses. Mollie didn't like getting up early in the morning, and tried to leave work early. Her usual excuse was: 'There's a stone in my hoof [5] — it hurts!'

Boxer was a real work champion. Whenever there was a problem, Boxer always said, 'I will work harder!' And he did. All the animals admired him. Benjamin the donkey seemed quite unchanged since the Rebellion. He did his work in his usual slow, silent way.

One day Boxer asked him, 'Benjamin, aren't you happier now that Mr Jones is gone?'

Benjamin's strange answer was, 'Donkeys live a long time. None of you have ever seen a dead donkey.'

There was no work on Sundays and breakfast was an hour later than usual. After breakfast there was the flag raising ceremony. Snowball found Mrs Jones's old green tablecloth and painted a hoof and a horn with white paint. The flag represented Animal Farm.

After raising the flag, everyone went to the weekly meeting. At the meeting the work of the coming week was planned and other things were discussed. However, the pigs were always the leaders. They planned everything. Napoleon and Snowball worked together but they never agreed on things.

In the old tool room, the pigs set up their offices. Here they studied and read books from the Jones farmhouse. Snowball worked busily and organized the Animal Committees. He set up the Egg Production Committee for the hens, the Clean Tails League for the cows, the Whiter Wool Movement for the sheep and several others. But these committees were not successful.

---

5. **hoof**: the hard covering on the feet of certain animals such as horses.

ACTIVITIES

The text and *beyond*

Comprehension check

1 **Choose the correct answer — a, b, c or d.**

1 Who learned to read and write?
   a ☐ All the pigs.
   b ☐ Mr Jones' children.
   c ☐ Boxer and Clover.
   d ☐ Napoleon, Snowball and Squealer.

2 What colour paint did Snowball use to write the Seven Commandments?
   a ☐ Green and white.
   b ☐ White.
   c ☐ White and red.
   d ☐ Black and green.

3 What happened to the five buckets of creamy milk?
   a ☐ They disappeared.
   b ☐ They were used in the feed for the hens.
   c ☐ Boxer and Clover drank them.
   d ☐ They were put in the storage shed.

4 Which farm animal lived a long time?
   a ☐ The goat.
   b ☐ The pig.
   c ☐ The donkey.
   d ☐ The sheep.

5 Where did the pigs set up their offices?
   a ☐ In Mr Jones farmhouse.
   b ☐ In the old tool room.
   c ☐ In the storage shed.
   d ☐ In the old hen-houses.

ACTIVITIES

Odd one out

2 A Circle the word that doesn't belong and explain why.

1 pig • donkey • sheep • raven
2 job • farmer • work • profession
3 delighted • pleased • happy • upset
4 novel • short story • biography • dictionary
5 England • British • France • United States
6 brave • frightened • scared • afraid

B Now circle the odd words in the word square.

C Complete the sentences with the odd words.

1 Mr Jones was a .... citizen.
2 The cows were .... fighters during the rebellion.
3 The .... flew into the barn at dawn.
4 The .... milked the cows every morning.
5 Mollie was .... because she didn't like to work.
6 The pigs found an English .... in the Jones house.

Culture Spot

B1 PRELIMINARY Read the text below and choose the correct answer.

The Society for the Prevention of Cruelty to Animals

In Great Britain, in 1824, Richard Martin founded the first Society for the Prevention of Cruelty to Animals, SPCA. People finally began to (**1**) .... that animals were living creatures with feelings; it was (**2**) .... wrong to mistreat them in any way. In 1840 Queen Victoria gave her (**3**) .... to call it the Royal Society for the Prevention of Cruelty to Animals. Today the RSPCA is active all over Great Britain.

In 1866, Henry Bergh opened the SPCA in New York City. He was a kind man who loved animals. He (**4**) .... that many masters were cruel and mistreated their animals. In 1867 there was the first ambulance for injured horses in New York City. Bergh later opened an animal hospital and several animal shelters.

Today the SPCA has animal hospitals and shelters all over the United States. It works with the American government to (**5**) .... laws that protect animals and improve their lives. Thanks to these laws, people from the SPCA visit zoos, national parks, pet shops, farms, circuses and homes to make sure the animals are treated well. They also go to schools to teach (**6**) .... towards all animals.

The SPCA shelters look after homeless animals and find them a loving home, and it has become an international organization.

1	a study	b assume	c summarise	d understand
2	a much	b many	c terribly	d terrible
3	a money	b permission	c idea	d permit
4	a noticed	b detected	c perceived	d regarded
5	a send	b do	c make	d build
6	a good	b well	c kindly	d kindness

ACTIVITIES

Internet project

Intensive farming vs. organic farming

Farming long ago was very different from farming today. In the 19th and 20th centuries the greater availability of pesticides,[1] herbicides[2] and other chemical products changed the way farmers grow crops.

How does this affect us and our planet? Surf the Net and find out more about intensive farming and organic farming.

1 Work with a partner and answer the following questions.

1. What is intensive farming?
2. What is organic farming?
3. What are the advantages and disadvantages of intensive farming?
4. Which kind of farming is sustainable[3] and more environmentally friendly?
5. What is food safety and why has it become more of a problem?
6. Which pesticides and herbicides are dangerous to our health?
7. What is animal welfare and why is it important?
8. Do you think farming in the future will be able to feed our growing world population?

---

1. **pesticides** : chemicals that farmers put on their crops to kill insects.
2. **herbicides** : chemicals used to destroy certain plants, especially wild plants.
3. **sustainable** : a system that respects and looks after the world's natural resources: the oceans, rivers, forests, land and air, because these resources must last for the future generations.

CHAPTER 4

NINE NEW PUPPIES

Snowball wanted the animals to learn to read and write, and these classes were a success. By the autumn many of the animals could read and write — some better than others. The pigs could already read and write perfectly. The dogs learned to read fairly well, but they were only interested in reading the Seven Commandments. Benjamin could read as well as the pigs, but he said that there was nothing worth reading. Clover learned the entire alphabet, but she couldn't put words together. Boxer could not get past the letter D. He often wrote the first four letters in the ground with his big hoof, but he didn't learn or remember the other letters.

'I'm happy with the first four letters,' he often told himself, staring at the A, B, C and D in the ground.

Mollie, the silly mare, once said, 'I only need to learn the letters of my name. They're the only important ones!'

CHAPTER 4

The stupider animals, like the sheep, hens and ducks were unable to learn the alphabet or the Seven Commandments by heart.

One old hen said, 'I want something easy to remember.'

'So do we!' cried the other hens and the sheep.

Clever Snowball replied, 'Very well, all you need to remember is this: FOUR LEGS GOOD, TWO LEGS BAD!'.

The birds were unhappy with this, so Snowball explained that they had two wings plus two legs — and that made four. This saved them! The sheep were very happy and they often lay in the field singing, 'Four legs good, two legs bad!' They kept on singing for hours.

Napoleon had no interest in Snowball's committees. He was interested in the education of the young because he considered it more important. One day he went to talk to the dogs, Jessie and Bluebell.

'Comrades, Jessie and Bluebell!' said Napoleon, cheerfully. 'Congratulations on your nine new puppies! They look clever and I want to educate them. Just think of how lucky they are!'

Jessie and Bluebell looked at each other and didn't know what to say. 'Yes, they're... lucky because you'll educate them.'

Napoleon took them away from their mothers and put them up on a high place in a corner of the barn. No one could reach it without a ladder that Napoleon always hid. The other animals forgot about the nine puppies.

Some of the animals noticed that the milk from the cows disappeared every day. They also noticed that the juicy apples that fell from the trees were not given to the animals, but were quickly brought to the pigs' offices. The animals started to think and ask questions, but Squealer explained the mystery brilliantly.

CHAPTER 4

'Comrades!' he cried. 'Please don't think that we pigs are taking the milk and the apples because we like them! No, no! We actually dislike them, but we take them to keep healthy and smart. Science has shown us that milk and apples are a necessary food for us pigs. They are brain foods and we pigs are brain workers. The whole management and organization of this farm depends on us. Day and night we watch over you to keep you safe and happy.' Squealer stopped for a moment and looked at the animals, moving his little tail.

Then he continued with an even louder voice. 'Do you know what would happen if we pigs didn't do our brain work? Well, I'll tell you: Mr Jones could come back! Yes! He could come back. Surely, none of you want Mr Jones to come back!' Squealer spoke excitedly, jumping back and forth.

All the animals agreed on this: they did not want Mr Jones! It was extremely important that the pigs remain in good health. So it was agreed that the milk and the apples were only for the pigs.

By the end of summer half the country knew about the rebellion at Manor Farm. Every day Snowball and Napoleon sent out pigeons to nearby farms. These pigeons told the other animals the story of the rebellion and taught them the tune of 'Beasts of England'.

Most of this time Mr Jones sat at the Red Lion Pub drinking and complaining about his bad luck. The other farmers listened and secretly thought: how can I take advantage of Jones's bad luck? The two nearby farms were called Foxwood and Pinchfield, and their owners were Mr Pilkington and Mr Frederick.

Mr Pilkington spent most of his time fishing or hunting and didn't look after Foxwood. As a result, his farm was in poor condition. Mr Frederick, however, was a tough, clever man and he looked after Pinchfield, a fine farm.

NINE NEW PUPPIES

The two farmers really disliked each other, but both of them were frightened by the rebellion on Animal Farm. They certainly didn't want their animals to learn too much about it. They started to tell stories about all the horrible things that happened to the poor animals at Manor Farm. They didn't want to use the new name, Animal Farm. They said that the animals were very hungry and they were killing each other.

However, the animals at Foxwood and Pinchfield didn't believe these stories.

A kind of rebellion ran through the countryside.

Bulls started to behave wildly, sheep broke the fences and didn't obey anyone, and cows kicked the milk buckets. All the animals on nearby farms knew the song 'Beasts of England' and sang it happily.

Of course, the farmers whipped these poor animals.

ACTIVITIES

The text and *beyond*

Comprehension check

1 Read the first part of each sentence (1-12) and match it with a conclusion (a-l).

1. ☐ The only animals
2. ☐ Mollie, the silly mare,
3. ☐ Napoleon went to see Jessie and Bluebell
4. ☐ The milk from the cows and the apples from the trees
5. ☐ Clever Squealer told the animals
6. ☐ The animals were very afraid
7. ☐ The pigeons flew to nearby farms
8. ☐ Foxwood farm was in poor condition
9. ☐ Mr Frederick was a clever man
10. ☐ Mr Pilkington and Mr Frederick told their animals stories
11. ☐ A kind of rebellion went through the countryside
12. ☐ The farmers on the nearby farms

a because he wanted to take their nine puppies away from them.
b that the pigs needed milk and apples because they were brain foods.
c because Mr Pilkington went fishing or hunting most of the time.
d and the animals on the other farms started to behave wildly.
e that Mr Jones could come back to the farm.
f that could read and write perfectly were the pigs.
g and he looked after his farm, Pinchfield.
h whipped the animals that sang the song 'Beasts of England'.
i and told the animals the story of the rebellion and taught them their song.
j about the terrible happenings at Animal Farm.
k only wanted to learn the letters of her name.
l were given to the brain workers, the pigs.

ACTIVITIES

So, neither, nor

> *One old hen said, 'I want something easy to remember.'*
> *'**So** do we!' cried the other hens and the sheep.*
>
> If you want to **agree with a positive statement**, use *so* + **auxiliary** + **subject pronoun**.
>
> *'I like visiting new places.' '**So** do I.'*
> *'My sister can play the piano.' '**So** can I.'*
>
> If you want to **agree with a negative statement**, use *neither/nor* + **auxiliary** + **subject pronoun**.
>
> *'I don't want to spend any money.' '**Neither** do I.'*
> *'We won't finish our homework today.' '**Nor** will we.'*
>
> **BE CAREFUL!**
>
> Remember to use the same auxiliary verb as in the sentence you are responding to.
>
> *'I don't have any pets.' '**Neither do** I.'*

Grammar: *so, neither, nor*

2 Match the statements with the correct answer. Each statement has one correct answer.

1. ☐ I have a new bicycle.
2. ☐ My father works on a farm.
3. ☐ I can't remember the name of that song.
4. ☐ We won't go to London today.
5. ☐ My brother can't speak French.
6. ☐ We went to the library yesterday.

a Neither can I.
b So does mine.
c Neither can mine.
d So did we.
e So do I.
f Nor will we.

ACTIVITIES

Before you read

Vocabulary

1 Match the words with their meanings. Use a dictionary if necessary.

1 ☐ to trample   3 ☐ to starve
2 ☐ to gallop   4 ☐ to whistle

a When a horse runs very fast.
b To make a sharp sound by forcing air between your lips.
c To suffer and sometimes die because you have no food.
d To step on a person's body violently, injuring or killing them; usually referred to animals.

2 Match the words with the correct picture.

1 geese   3 windmill
2 brass medal   4 horseshoe

 A ☐
 B ☐
 C ☐
 D ☐

Listening

3 Listen to the first part of Chapter 5 and decide if the sentences below are true (T) or false (F). Correct the false ones.

		T	F
1	Mr Jones took his gun and went to fight by himself.	☐	☐
2	Snowball was ready for the attack because he studied the battles of Julius Caesar.	☐	☐
3	Mr Jones shot his gun and killed a pig.	☐	☐
4	Boxer fought very bravely during the attack.	☐	☐

CHAPTER 5

BATTLE OF THE COWSHED

All the farmers were terribly afraid of a rebellion on their farms. So, they decided to get together and fight. Mr Jones wanted to go back to his farm. One October morning he and his men joined six or seven other men from Foxwood and Pinchfield.

'Get your biggest sticks¹ ready,' cried Mr Jones to the other men. 'I'm going to take my gun! Manor Farm is mine. Let's go and fight! Let's show them that we men are their masters! They won't rebel again!'

In the meantime, the pigeons came flying through the air and warned the pigs that Mr Jones and other men were coming.

Snowball was ready for the attack and said, 'Comrades, listen

---

1. **big stick** : (here)

CHAPTER 5

carefully! Some time ago I found an old book at the Jones' farmhouse. It talked about the famous Roman emperor, Julius Caesar. During these months I've studied the famous battles of Julius Caesar and I've learned a lot! The Romans invaded almost all of Europe and with Julius Caesar's knowledge we will win against our common enemy: man!'

Snowball gave his orders quickly and in a few minutes every animal was ready for the battle. When Mr Jones and his angry men approached the farm buildings, Snowball began his first attack.

'Pigeons! Attack now!' cried Snowball. Thirty-five angry pigeons flew over the heads of the men and dirtied them. As the men were cleaning their heads, the geese attacked and bit their legs.

Then Snowball shouted, 'Muriel, Benjamin, sheep: let's go forward and fight!' Snowball led these angry animals that butted and kicked the men. But the men with their big sticks made the animals run back into the yard.

'Hurrah! Hurrah!' shouted the men as they ran into the yard with their sticks in their hands. This was just what Snowball wanted. As soon as the men were inside the yard, the three horses, the three cows and the other pigs attacked from the back! This was a shock for the men. Mr Jones shot his gun and a sheep fell dead. Snowball's back was injured.

The most terrifying part of the battle was Boxer with his giant hoofs. He was dangerous as he kicked and trampled the men. Every animal on the farm fought bravely, even the cat! A few minutes later the men were running away, frightened, but a young boy lay face down in the grass.

'He's dead,' said Boxer sadly. 'I didn't want to hurt him! My iron horseshoes are terribly heavy. I am truly sorry...'

CHAPTER 5

Snowball's back was covered with blood and he said, 'War is war, comrade! The only good human being is a dead one.'

'But I didn't want to kill him,' Boxer said, with tears in his big eyes.

'Where's Mollie?' asked one of the cows.

The animals went to look for her and found her hiding in her stall.[2] She hid there when she heard Mr Jones's gun. When the others went back to the yard, the young boy was gone. He was probably feeling better and ran away.

The animals had a wild victory celebration. The flag went up and 'Beasts of England' was sung many times. The animals decided to create a military decoration 'Animal Hero First Class' that was given to Snowball and Boxer. They were old brass medals found in the tool room. There was also 'Animal Hero, Second Class', that was given to the dead sheep. The victorious battle was named the Battle of the Cowshed.

In December Mollie was always late for work and liked going to the fields. So, Clover decided to talk to her.

'Mollie, this morning I saw you in the fields. You were talking to a man from Foxwood. Why?'

Mollie answered nervously, 'That's not true, Clover! Not true!' She turned around and galloped away. Three days later she disappeared, and the pigeons said they had seen her pulling a red and black cart, and she had a red ribbon on her head. No one ever talked about Mollie again.

In January the weather was terribly cold. No one could work in the fields. There were several meetings in the big barn and Snowball and Napoleon always argued. They disagreed on everything.

---

2. **stall** : a separate space in a barn for a horse.

BATTLE OF THE COWSHED

Snowball had many excellent ideas to improve the farm. But Napoleon was against all of them, especially the idea of a windmill.

'Comrades!' said Snowball, happily. 'There's a hill on the farm that is the perfect place for a windmill.'

'A what?' asked the animals, confused.

'A windmill is something wonderful! With the power of the wind we can have electricity on our farm. Electricity can do many useful things. With electricity there will be light in your stalls, and heat during the cold winter months. We can have an electric milking machine for the cows and a big machine to cut the hay! Comrades, you will all work less and be more comfortable. With less work you can have more free time to rest, read and talk!'

The animals listened to Snowball, amazed. Most of them did not understand the idea of a windmill, but he was a pig and pigs were smart! Most of the animals trusted them. Snowball worked on plans for the windmill and made excellent drawings of the project on the wooden floor of his office. He used a big piece of white chalk. The details for the windmill came from Mr Jones's books: *Electricity for Beginners* and *One Thousand Useful Things to do about the House*.

The animals went to look at Snowball's drawings at least once a day and were excited about the project. But Napoleon was not interested. One day he went to Snowball's office, looked at the plans, walked all over them and left angrily. He was jealous of Snowball. The entire farm was deeply divided on the project of the windmill.

'It will take a lot of hard work to build the windmill,' said Snowball, very honestly. 'We will need big stones to build the walls, and then we must make the...'

CHAPTER 5

'It's a huge waste of time!' cried Napoleon, nervously. 'We need to produce more food or we will starve!' Snowball and Napoleon also disagreed on many other things.

When Snowball's plan was completed, there was a meeting in the big barn on Sunday. The animals had to decide if they wanted to build the windmill or not. Snowball spoke first.

'Comrades! Vote for the windmill! It will make your lives much easier...' He went on to explain the advantages. Then Napoleon spoke.

'Comrades, the windmill is nonsense — pure nonsense! Don't vote for it!'

However, Snowball was an excellent speaker and he started to talk to the animals again. He was excited and he convinced the animals to vote for the windmill. When Napoleon realized that the animals wanted the windmill, he stood up and whistled in a very strange way.

The text and *beyond*

Comprehension check

1 Choose the correct answer — a, b, c or d.

1 The farmers in the area got together to attack Animal Farm
   a ☐ because they were good friends.
   b ☐ because they wanted to take Mr Jones's farm from him.
   c ☐ because they were afraid of a rebellion on their farms.
   d ☐ and they won the battle.

2 Who studied Julius Caesar's famous battle plans?
   a ☐ Snowball.
   b ☐ Napoleon.
   c ☐ Squealer.
   d ☐ Boxer.

3 The hill on the farm was
   a ☐ a dangerous place.
   b ☐ the perfect place for a vegetable garden.
   c ☐ the perfect place for a windmill.
   d ☐ the perfect place for the new hay field.

4 Snowball told the animals that
   a ☐ they will all get a military decoration.
   b ☐ Mollie must leave Animal Farm.
   c ☐ they must work longer hours.
   d ☐ the windmill was something wonderful.

5 When Napoleon realized that the animals wanted to vote for Snowball's idea,
   a ☐ he finally agreed on it.
   b ☐ he stood up and whistled in a strange way.
   c ☐ he got angry and walked out of the meeting.
   d ☐ he decided to leave Animal Farm.

Crossword puzzle

2 Have fun with this crossword puzzle!

ACROSS

3   A very young horse.
4   To kill animals to sell their meat.
8   Iron shoe a horse wears on its foot.
10 When a horse runs very fast.

DOWN

1   A building that uses the wind to make electricity.
2   Determined; not easy to get along with.
5   A violent, organized action by people who want to change a social system.
6   Female horse.
7   To step on the body of a person and injure the person.
9   To look at for a long time.

ACTIVITIES

Before you read

Speaking – Wind farms

1 **Read the text and discuss with your classmates.**

> Snowball told the animals about the power of the wind and the windmill. The power of the wind has been a friend to man for centuries because it created energy. This energy was used to do many things. The wind is a renewable source of energy. It is free, and it does not pollute the environment with CO_2 and other gases. Today we have wind farms. The tall, thin towers are called wind turbines and the blades of the turbines are moved by the wind to create energy and electricity.

1 Are there any wind farms in your country?
2 What other kinds of 'clean and renewable energy' do you know?

Vocabulary

2 **Match the words with their meanings. Use a dictionary if necessary.**

1 ☐ bark
2 ☐ fierce
3 ☐ obedience
4 ☐ discipline
5 ☐ sly
6 ☐ tactics
7 ☐ voluntary
8 ☐ quarry

a Very clever but not very honest, and difficult to trust.
b A place on the side of a mountain where you can always find big stones.
c The sound dogs make.
d Clever methods used to achieve something you want.
e Strict training, orderly standards of behaviour.
f When you do what you are told to do.
g Dangerous, wild, cruel.
h Something you do because you want to do it, not because you are forced to do it.

CHAPTER **6**

A SURPRISING ANNOUNCEMENT

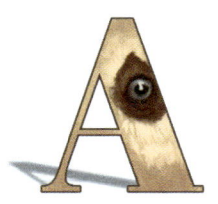

A few moments after Napoleon's strange whistle, nine enormous dogs ran into the barn. They were barking loudly and wanted to attack Snowball. Poor Snowball was terribly frightened and ran out of the barn. The nine dogs followed him closely and one dog bit his tail. He ran very fast and was able to escape through a hole in the stone wall. Snowball disappeared and no one ever saw him again! The animals were silent and terrified.

'Where did those nine fierce dogs come from?' asked a young pig.

'They were our puppies!' said Jessie, looking at Bluebell sadly. 'Napoleon took them away from us and... educated them.'

Now that Snowball was gone, Napoleon was satisfied.

He stood in front of the animals, with the dogs near him, and said,

A SURPRISING ANNOUNCEMENT

'There will be no more Sunday meetings! They are unnecessary. All matters about farm work will be decided by a special committee of pigs that I will choose. We will make all the decisions. And on Sunday mornings, after raising the flag and singing 'Beasts of England', you will receive your work orders for the week.'

The animals were quite annoyed and angry. Even Boxer was bothered by these decisions. Four young pigs stood up and complained loudly. But suddenly the fierce dogs started to bark and the pigs were silent and sat down. Afterwards Squealer went around the farm to explain things to the animals.

'Comrades,' he said, 'I'm sure that every animal understands the hard work that Comrade Napoleon is doing for us. Don't think that leadership is a pleasure! No, no! It is a terribly heavy responsibility. Napoleon could let you make your decisions by yourselves, but you could easily make the wrong decisions! Suppose you decided to build Snowball's windmill — just think! What a big mistake! Snowball was no better than a criminal!'

'He fought bravely at the Battle of the Cowshed,' said a cow.

'Bravery is not enough,' said Squealer. 'Obedience is more important. Discipline, comrades, discipline is the right word! If we make one mistake, just one — Jones will come back! Remember!'

Boxer had time to think about Squealer's speech and said, 'If Comrade Napoleon says it, it must be right.' And from then on he always said, 'Napoleon is always right', in addition to 'I will work harder'.

Three weeks after Snowball's disappearance, Napoleon made a surprising announcement.

'Comrades, I have decided to build the windmill. It will be a very difficult job. There will probably be less food for everyone. It will take about two years of extremely hard work.'

CHAPTER 6

Napoleon did not explain why he changed his mind. But sly Squealer went around to talk to the animals. 'Comrades, let me explain why Napoleon wants to build the windmill. Comrade Napoleon was never against the windmill. Actually, it was his idea, not Snowball's! Snowball stole Napoleon's plans!'

'But why did he speak against the windmill? I don't understand,' asked a goat.

Squealer was not only sly, he was very clever. He answered, 'Napoleon seemed against the windmill because he wanted to get rid of Snowball. You all know that Snowball was a dangerous character and a bad example for the other animals. With Snowball gone, the plan can go on. You see, this is called tactics — tactics!' He jumped around happily and laughed, 'Tactics, comrades, tactics!'

The animals did not really understand the meaning of the word, but Squealer was very convincing. And the three dogs that were with Squealer barked angrily, and so the animals accepted his explanation without other questions. They worked like slaves that year. However, they were happy because they knew the windmill was for them, and not for the selfish human beings.

In August Napoleon announced, 'Comrades, we must work harder, so there will be voluntary work on Sunday afternoons. However, if an animal does not volunteer, he or she will receive less food!'

As everyone was working on the windmill, the harvest was less successful than the previous year. The windmill was difficult to build for many reasons. It was impossible for the animals to use certain tools that were made for humans. Stones were needed to make the walls. However, the stones were in a faraway quarry and they were heavy and huge. The animals needed to bring them up the hill to the area of the future windmill.

CHAPTER 6

Boxer was the best and strongest worker. He never complained and pushed the huge stones up the hill from the quarry.

Clover was worried about Boxer because the work was exhausting. 'Boxer, please don't work too much! You look very tired! Take a rest — go slowly.'

Boxer's answer was, 'I will work harder! Napoleon is always right!' He asked one of the birds to wake him up forty-five minutes earlier than the others, because he wanted to work more.

Towards the end of the summer, Napoleon made an important announcement one Sunday morning. 'I have decided that Animal Farm will start to trade with other farms. Of course, this is not for any business purpose or to make money. No, no! It is simply to get the materials that are necessary for the windmill. The building of the windmill is our most important project!'

'But we have always been against working with human beings and against making money,' said one of the four young pigs. 'We made those rules when Mr Jones left the farm!'

'Yes!' agreed the other animals. 'We remember... or at least. we think we remember.'

Suddenly, Napoleon's fierce dogs barked at the young pigs and they were silent. Then the sheep started to say, 'Four legs good, two legs bad!'

Napoleon raised his trotter for silence and announced, 'I will contact the human beings — a very difficult and unpleasant job, but I must do it!'

Mr Whymper was an unimportant lawyer in the town of Willingdon, but he was a sly man. He became the agent between Animal Farm and the outside world. He knew he could make money in this way.

After Napoleon's surprising announcement, sly Squealer went

A SURPRISING ANNOUNCEMENT

to talk to the animals. 'We have never been against working with human beings, or against making money! No, no! You don't remember! It's your imagination — a dream, perhaps! Snowball probably told you those terrible lies!'

The sheep looked at each other and said, 'It's our mistake; we didn't remember correctly...'

The hens cried, 'It was certainly a dream... only a dream.'

The cows looked confused and said, 'Ah... our mistake.'

Once again, Squealer's cleverness convinced the animals.

ACTIVITIES

The text and *beyond*

Comprehension check

1 Answer the following questions.

1. Why do you think nine fierce dogs chased Snowball out of Animal Farm?
2. What happened to the four young pigs that complained loudly?
3. Why did Squealer say that Napoleon had to make the decisions?
4. How did Squealer explain Napoleon's decision to build the windmill?
5. Why were the animals happy to work like slaves on the windmill?
6. How did Napoleon convince the animals to do the 'voluntary' work?
7. Why was it difficult to build the windmill?
8. Who was Mr Whymper and why did Napoleon need to contact him?
9. How did Squealer convince the animals that they had never been against working with human beings?

Sentence transformation

2 For each question, complete the second sentence so that it means the same as the first. Use no more than three words.

1. Mr Frederick lived alone on his farm.
   Mr Frederick .... with anyone.
2. Are these Mr Jones's tools?
   Do these tools .... Mr Jones?
3. It was so dark that he couldn't see the road.
   It was .... see the road.
4. How much does the corn cost?
   What's .... of the corn?
5. It's not safe to cross the river during the storm.
   It's .... the river during the storm.

ACTIVITIES

Notices

3 **B1 PRELIMINARY** Look at the following notices. What do they say? Choose the correct answer.

1

RED LION PUB
Since 1684
Service with a smile.
Open all year – We close at 2 pm on Christmas Day.
Hot soup lunch every day at noon.
Meat pie dinner every evening from 6 to 7 pm.

a ☐ You can eat meat pie here on Christmas Day.
b ☐ We are friendly people.
c ☐ You can have hot soup from 6 to 7 pm.

2

SIMON'S HORSE CART SHOP
Open from 8 am to 5 pm – closed at weekends.
Repairs take 4 working days if you bring the cart before noon, otherwise repairs take 5 days.
All work must be paid in advance.

a ☐ Repairs are always done at noon.
b ☐ You must pay before we do the repair work.
c ☐ All repairs take 5 days.

3

WILLINGDON Train Station
The 8 am Sunday train to London has been cancelled during the winter.
On rainy days trains to London leave from Platform 3 instead of Platform 1.
All trains to Liverpool leave from Platform 2 at weekends.

a ☐ In January you can't go to London by train on Sunday mornings.
b ☐ When you go to London, always use Platform 1 on rainy days.
c ☐ You can't take the train to Liverpool from Platform 2 on Tuesdays.

4

MISS PRIM'S OLD CURIOSITY SHOP
Open afternoons only from 2 pm to 6 pm.
We buy and sell books, furniture, old toys, used tools and useful objects of all kinds.

a ☐ You can shop here in the morning.
b ☐ You can sell your old chairs here.
c ☐ Everything in the shop is cheap.

ACTIVITIES

Before you read

Listening

1 Listen to Chapter 7 and choose the correct answer.

1 Where did the pigs go to live?

A

B

C

2 What was the weather like one night late in November?

A

B

C

3 How many eggs did Mr Whymper want each week?

340   **40**   **400**

A   B   C

4 Which animals died because they were without food?

A

B

C

CHAPTER 7

THE NOVEMBER STORM

Every Monday Mr Whymper visited the farm and talked to Napoleon. The animals avoided him as much as possible, but when they saw Napoleon on four legs giving orders to Mr Whymper on two legs, they felt proud. The people in Willingdon and the nearby farmers hated Animal Farm and were certain that the windmill could never work. Mr and Mrs Jones went to live in another part of England.

One day the pigs suddenly moved into the farmhouse — the farmhouse that belonged to Mr Jones!

When this happened, many animals began to complain. 'There was a rule or an agreement that no animal could live in the house of a human,' said a goat, and the animals agreed with him.

Clever Squealer heard the complaints and said, 'Oh, comrades, you don't understand! It's absolutely necessary that the pigs

CHAPTER 7

have a quiet place to work. After all, the pigs are the brains of our farm. And Napoleon is our Leader and leaders must live in a nice, comfortable place.'

Napoleon was suddenly called their Leader.

However, some animals were very annoyed when they heard that the pigs ate in the kitchen, sat in the comfortable sitting room and slept in the beds! Clover remembered that there was a rule against beds. She went to the end of the barn and tried to read the Seven Commandments, but she was unable to read them. She called Muriel, the goat.

'Muriel, please read me the Fourth Commandment. Doesn't it say: No animal shall sleep in a bed?'

Muriel read it slowly, 'No animal shall sleep in a bed with sheets.'

'Oh, I didn't' remember the part about the sheets,' said Clover. 'If it's written on the wall...'

At that moment Squealer was walking by with his three dogs. 'Comrades, you already know that we pigs now sleep in beds at the farmhouse. And why not? There is no rule against beds! A bed means a place where you sleep. The straw in your stalls is a bed. The rule was against sheets because they are a human invention. We pigs have removed the sheets and we sleep between blankets. We need our sleep with all the brainwork that we do. If we are tired, we can't do our brainwork. And I'm sure you don't want Jones to come back!'

A few days later it was announced that the pigs could get up an hour later than the other animals. No one complained about this announcement.

The harvest went quite well and a good part of the corn and hay were sold. The work on the windmill continued through the summer and autumn.

THE NOVEMBER STORM

The animals were tired but satisfied, because the windmill was half built now. They were proud of their hard work.

One night late in November there were extremely strong winds that shook the barn and the farmhouse. The next morning the animals left the barn and saw something terrible: 'The windmill has been destroyed,' said one of the young pigs. This sight shocked the animals.

Napoleon ran out of the farmhouse and looked at the windmill in ruins. At first he couldn't speak and then he started to smell the ground near the ruins of the windmill.

Suddenly Napoleon shouted, 'Comrades, do you know who is responsible for this? Do you know the enemy who came last night to destroy our windmill? Snowball! Snowball is our enemy! And now there is a death sentence on Snowball! I will give an Animal Hero, Second Class medal and a half bucket full of apples to any animal that brings him here dead! And a full bucket of apples to any animal that brings him here alive! However, comrades, our work must continue during the winter. No one can stop our windmill!'

The animals were deeply shocked. How could Snowball possibly do such an awful thing? Muriel said, 'What a terrible enemy we have! We must find Snowball and get the prize!' The animals began to think of ways of finding their enemy.

It was an extremely cold winter. The stormy weather of November was followed by ice and snow. The animals worked as hard as possible, but they were always cold and hungry. Only Boxer and Clover never complained. Squealer gave excellent speeches about the happiness and satisfaction of hard work.

In January there was very little food left and Animal Farm was close to starvation.

CHAPTER 7

The poor animals struggled with cold and hunger, and yet they continued to work on the windmill. Napoleon rarely appeared in public and when he did, he was followed by six fierce dogs.

One Sunday morning in spring, Squealer announced that the hens must give all their eggs to Mr Whymper. Napoleon had a contract with him for four hundred eggs a week because he needed money to buy grain. The hens were very angry.

'We can't give away our eggs now,' said one hen angrily. 'It's spring and it's time for the baby chicks to be born. It's terribly cruel!'

There was a lot of trouble in the hen house and there was a hen rebellion. Napoleon didn't give the hens any more food. For five days they were without food and nine of them died. On the sixth day the other hens had to give their eggs to Mr Whymper, who delivered them to the grocer each week.

Early in the spring a strange rumour[1] went around Animal Farm: Snowball was secretly visiting the farm every night! Whenever something went wrong or something broke, it was always Snowball's fault. Most of the animals believed this rumour, and even the cows said that Snowball milked them during their sleep.

One evening Squealer spoke to the animals in his usual sly way. 'Comrades, we pigs have discovered something terrible: Snowball was Jones's secret agent all the time! We found documents that clearly show this! He didn't want us to win the Battle of the Cowshed!'

The animals were shocked when they heard this. It took them a few minutes to understand this awful news. Boxer rarely asked questions but this time, slowly, he said, 'I do not believe this!'

---

1. **rumour** : things that the animals say; gossip.

CHAPTER 7

'Snowball fought bravely at the Battle of the Cowshed. Didn't we give him the "Animal Hero, First Class" medal?'

'That was our mistake, comrade!' said Squealer. 'Now we know that he was Jones's secret agent. It's all written in the secret documents. Besides, our Leader Comrade Napoleon said that Snowball was Jones's agent.'

Boxer thought for a moment and said, 'Ah, if Comrade Napoleon said it, it must be right.'

'Good! Now you understand!' said Squealer, looking at Boxer angrily. 'We think there are some of Snowball's secret agents among us right now! Be careful and keep your eyes open!'

ACTIVITIES

The text and *beyond*

Comprehension check

1 Choose the correct answer — a, b, c or d.

1   The animals felt proud because
    a ☐ Mr and Mrs Jones went to live faraway.
    b ☐ Mr Whymper visited Animal Farm every Monday.
    c ☐ Napoleon gave orders to Mr Whymper.
    d ☐ they made friends with Mr Whymper.

2   Clover remembered that there was a rule against
    a ☐ sleeping in beds.
    b ☐ eating in a kitchen.
    c ☐ sitting on the sofa of a sitting room.
    d ☐ bed sheets.

3   One November night the windmill was destroyed by
    a ☐ Snowball.
    b ☐ very strong winds.
    c ☐ Mr Jones and his helpers.
    d ☐ the people of Willingdon.

4   In the cold month of January the animals were close to starvation
    a ☐ but Squealer gave speeches about the happiness and satisfaction of hard work.
    b ☐ and Napoleon gave each animal a half bucket of apples.
    c ☐ and half of them died.
    d ☐ and all of them stopped working on the windmill.

5   There was a hen rebellion because
    a ☐ they wanted a bigger and warmer hen-house.
    b ☐ they didn't like Mr Whymper.
    c ☐ they didn't want to give away their eggs in the spring.
    d ☐ they wanted more food.

Culture Spot

B1 PRELIMINARY Five sentences have been removed from the text below. For each question, choose the correct answer. There are three extra sentences which you do not need to use.

Ravens

In the story you are reading, Moses is a raven. Ravens are big black birds that look like crows, but they are much bigger. They are very intelligent. They like playing together and making funny noises. They usually travel in pairs. (**1**) .... The most famous raven is probably the one in Edgar Allen Poe's poem, *The Raven*. (**2**) ....

The raven is a very important bird in Great Britain, and particularly in London. An old legend says that if the ravens leave the Tower of London, the kingdom will fall! No one knows exactly when the ravens came to the Tower of London, but they are welcome there. Today seven ravens live at the Tower of London. (**3**) .... To stop the ravens from leaving, some of their feathers are taken from their wings so that they can't fly away. A man called the Ravenmaster looks after them every day. He feeds them meat and biscuits. During the day they are free to move around. (**4**) .... Ravens usually live about 40 years. Thousands of tourists visit the Tower of London every year. (**5**) .... These wonderful black birds have become a great tourist attraction.

- **A** They love taking pictures and videos of the ravens.
- **B** There are several tourist guides at the Tower of London.
- **C** At night they sleep in special cages.
- **D** The Ravenmaster loves all animals.
- **E** These birds love their family and protect their young.
- **F** It's a mysterious and rather frightening poem about a raven who is a messenger.
- **G** Each one of them has a name.
- **H** Edgar Allen Poe kept a raven as a pet.

CHAPTER **8**

THE BANKNOTES[1]

Late one afternoon Napoleon ordered all the animals to meet in the big yard. His nine fierce dogs were there, too, and he was wearing both his medals. 'We have just found some of Snowball's secret agents here at Animal Farm, and now we will hear their confessions[2] and punish them.' The animals didn't quite understand what was happening, but they were silent. The fierce dogs went to get four of the pigs that always complained and pulled them by the ear to Napoleon's feet.

Napoleon said that they had to confess their crimes. The four pigs were terrified and confessed: they were Snowball's secret agents and they helped him to destroy the windmill.

---

1. **banknote**: paper money.
2. **confession**: the act of saying that you did something wrong, embarrassing or illegal.

CHAPTER 8

When they finished, the fierce dogs attacked and killed them.

The dogs then attacked and killed the three hens that started the egg rebellion. The two sheep that said bad things about Napoleon were also attacked and killed. The last victim was the goose that complained too much. The bloody bodies of the animals lay at Napoleon's feet. The air was heavy with the smell of blood. The animals could not speak. They were shocked and terrified, and slowly went to the hill where the half-finished windmill stood.

The animals looked at Boxer and Clover but no one spoke.

Finally Boxer said, 'I do not understand what is happening. How can such terrible things happen here? Perhaps it's our fault — we must work harder! I must work harder.'

Clover's eyes were full of tears and she could not speak. But she thought, 'This is not what we animals wanted! Old Major promised a farm that was free from hunger, cruelty and terror. Now we are afraid to speak and we cannot disagree with our leader. We are not equal anymore. But perhaps things are better now than in the days of Jones and his men... I don't know! I can only work hard and obey Napoleon, our leader.'

Then Clover began to sing 'Beasts of England' and the other animals joined her. Suddenly Squealer appeared accompanied by two fierce dogs. 'Comrade Napoleon has just announced that it is forbidden to sing "Beats of England".'

Muriel was surprised and asked, 'Why?'

'It was the song of the Rebellion,' replied Squealer, coldly. 'But the Rebellion is over. We have killed our enemies, the secret agents. Now we have a perfect society.'

A few days after the killings, some of the animals remembered, or thought they remembered, the Sixth Commandment:

'No animal shall kill any other animal.'

THE BANKNOTES

Clover asked Muriel to read the Sixth Commandment:
'No animal shall kill any other animal without cause.'

Somehow the last two words were not in the animals' memory. However, now it was clear that there was a good reason to kill those animals as they were enemies.

During the year the animals worked even harder than the year before. They had to build the windmill and harvest the crops. The walls of the windmill were twice as thick as before and this needed a great amount of work.

Napoleon was rarely seen in public. When he appeared, a black rooster[3] walked in front of him and let out a loud 'cock-a-doodle-do' before he spoke. The fierce dogs were always with him, too. He lived in separate rooms from the others, and took his meals alone with two dogs to serve him. He used the best dishes from the cupboard.

The pigs invented names for him like Father of All Animals, Terror of Mankind or Protector of the Sheep. Squealer often spoke of Napoleon's good heart and deep love for all animals everywhere.

With Mr Whymper's help, Napoleon was involved in a complicated business with Mr Frederick and Mr Pilkington, from the nearby farms. There was a big pile of wood to sell and both Frederick and Pilkington wanted to buy it. However, Napoleon did not want to sell it to Frederick because he was considered an enemy of Animal Farm. There were rumours that he wanted to attack Animal Farm. It seemed that Pilkington was friendly with Napoleon. At the same time, there were rumours of a plan to kill Napoleon. The three hens that seemed to know about the

---

3. **rooster:**

CHAPTER 8

plan were immediately killed. Napoleon's safety became a serious problem. Four dogs guarded Napoleon's bed at night, and Pinkeye, a young pig, tasted Napoleon's food before he ate it. Napoleon was afraid that someone could put poison[4] in his food.

By the autumn the windmill was finally finished and the animals were very proud of their success. They walked around it and admired its beauty. The machinery was not there yet, but it was Mr Whymper's job to buy it. Napoleon himself came to admire the completed work and announced that the mill's name was Napoleon Mill.

Two days later, during a special meeting at the barn, the animals were very surprised to hear Napoleon announce, 'Today I sold the pile of wood to Frederick, and tomorrow Frederick's men will come and take it away.'

It seemed that Napoleon was friendly with Pilkington, but it was simply a tactic to increase the price of the wood. Napoleon had a secret agreement with Frederick, and so now Pilkington became the real enemy of Animal Farm. And it was discovered that Snowball was living in luxury at Foxwood Farm with Pilkington!

The pigs admired the superior quality of Napoleon's mind. Squealer told the animals, 'Frederick wanted to pay for the wood with something called a cheque, that is simply a piece of paper that says "I will pay you." But our Leader, Comrade Napoleon, is very clever and said that he wanted real money — five-pound notes, and not a cheque! So Frederick gave him the banknotes and then his men could take the wood away. That money will be used to buy the machinery for Napoleon Mill.' The animals listened carefully to Squealer.

---

4. **poison** : a substance that can harm or kill you if you eat or drink it.

CHAPTER 8

The day after a special meeting was held in the barn to show the animals Frederick's banknotes. Napoleon, with his medals, was on the platform on a bed of straw, with the pile of money on a fancy dish by his side. The animals walked by slowly and looked at the pile of money in amazement.

But three days later something terrible happened. Mr Whymper came up the path on his bicycle and ran into the farmhouse. A few minutes later, a loud cry of anger came from the farmhouse. The banknotes were forgeries![4] Frederick got the wood for nothing!

Napoleon was furious and immediately announced a terrible death sentence on Frederick. He warned the animals that Frederick and his men could attack at any time.

---

4. **forgery** : (here) a fake banknote with no value.

ACTIVITIES

The text and *beyond*

Comprehension check

1 Match the beginnings of the sentences (1-10) to their endings (a-j).

1. During a meeting in the big yard, Napoleon said
2. Napoleon wanted to hear their confessions
3. The fierce dogs
4. Clover was very upset and didn't speak,
5. Squealer told the animals that it was forbidden to sing 'Beasts of England',
6. Muriel read the Sixth Commandment
7. With Mr Whymper's help
8. The windmill was finished in the autumn
9. Napoleon sold a pile of wood to Mr Frederick
10. Napoleon wanted five-pound banknotes,

a but she remembered that Old Major promised a better life for the animals.
b and she saw two words that she didn't remember.
c because the rebellion was over and their society was perfect.
d but Mr Frederick wanted to pay Napoleon with a cheque.
e and so the four terrified pigs had to confess.
f but Mr Frederick gave him forgeries!
g and the animals were proud of their success.
h that some of Snowball's secret agents were at Animal Farm.
i killed the pigs and some other animals in a terrible way.
j Napoleon started business dealings with nearby farmers.

ACTIVITIES

Direct and reported Speech

*Napoleon **said that** they had to confess their crimes.*

In English there are two ways of **presenting what a person says**.
You can use the exact same words a person says: this is called **direct speech**.
When you report what a person says, you use **reported speech**.
Look at the sentences below and notice the changes in verbs, pronouns and possessive adjectives.

Direct speech	Reported speech
'Napoleon is talking to Snowball,' said Squealer.	Squealer said that Napoleon was talking to Snowball.
'The foals often gallop in the fields,' said Clover.	Clover said that the foals often galloped in the fields.
'I've lived on this farm for many years,' said Benjamin.	Benjamin said that he had lived on this farm for many years.
'I'm going to work hard on the windmill,' said Boxer.	Boxer said that he was going to work hard on the windmill.

Grammar: direct and reported speech

2 **A** Change the direct speech into reported speech.

1. 'The farmhouse is near the barn,' said Muriel.
2. 'Mr Jones is going to the pub,' said Mr Frederick.
3. 'The hens are going to the Sunday meeting,' said Bluebell.
4. 'Boxer has already been to the quarry to get the stones,' said Clover.

B Change the reported speech into direct speech.

1. Napoleon said that Boxer was the best worker.
2. Mollie said that she couldn't find her red ribbon.
3. Mr Whymper said that Mr Jones had always had dinner at six.
4. Clover said that her foal was playing in the grassy field.

ACTIVITIES

Before you read

Vocabulary

1 Match the words with their meanings. Use a dictionary if necessary.

1 ☐ barley
2 ☐ retire
3 ☐ brewing and distilling
4 ☐ whisky

a The processes of making beer and making whisky.
b An alcoholic drink.
c (here) To stop working because you are old.
d A plant that is used to make beer, whisky and some foods.

2 Match each word with the correct picture.

1 bullet
2 explosives
3 mug
4 parades

A

B

C

D

Listening

track 11

3 Listen to Chapter 9 and decide if the sentences below are true (T) or false (F). Correct the false ones.

		T	F
1	Frederick and nine men came through the big gate.	☐	☐
2	A terrible explosion destroyed the barn and henhouses.	☐	☐
3	Squealer said that the animals could rebuild several windmills.	☐	☐
4	Boxer's hoof hurt a lot and he decided to retire immediately.	☐	☐
5	The pigs and the dogs always had more food than the other animals.	☐	☐

75

CHAPTER **9**

EXPLOSIVES!

The next morning the attack came. The animals were having breakfast when three pigeons flew into the barn with the horrible news: Frederick and his men were coming through the big gate! There were fifteen angry men with six guns and they started shooting as soon as they entered. The bullets from the guns were flying everywhere and many of the animals were injured. They ran to the barn and shut the doors, but they could see what was happening outside. When Benjamin saw Frederick's men approaching the windmill he shouted, 'Those men are putting explosives around the windmill!'

The animals were terrified and waited inside the barn. After a few minutes the men ran away and there was a strong explosion. A cloud of black smoke surrounded the hill, and the windmill did not exist anymore! When the animals saw this terrible sight, their courage returned.

EXPLOSIVES!

They were no longer afraid and ran out of the barn and attacked the men. It was a horrible battle because a cow, three sheep, and two geese were killed and nearly everyone was injured. Boxer broke the heads of three men with his strong hoofs and others were wounded by the cows and the dogs. Frederick told his men to leave the farm immediately.

The animals won but they were wounded and very sad: their windmill was gone. However, Squealer insisted that this was a big victory and that the animals could easily rebuild the windmill, even several windmills. For the first time Boxer realized that he was eleven years old and rebuilding the windmill was going to be extremely hard. However, Napoleon proudly announced, 'We will celebrate our victory and call this the Battle of the Windmill.'

A few days later the pigs discovered many bottles of whisky in the cellar of the farmhouse. That evening there was loud singing at the farmhouse and Napoleon was running around the yard with Mr Jones's old bowler hat[1] on his head! The next day all was silent at the farmhouse and the pigs were not seen anywhere. Then Napoleon told Mr Whymper to buy some books on brewing and distilling. After reading these books, Napoleon decided to grow barley in the garden, as barley was needed to make whisky and beer. One day Muriel went to read the Seven Commandments to herself, and she noticed a change in the Fifth Commandment. Now it read: 'No animal shall drink alcohol TO EXCESS.'

The day after the victory celebrations the animals started to rebuild the windmill. Boxer was eleven years old and he was tired, but he wanted to work every day.

---

1. **bowler hat** :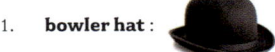

CHAPTER 9

One evening he told Clover, 'My hoof hurts a lot, and my legs aren't strong anymore. And I can't breathe well.'

'Boxer, you don't need to work so hard,' Clover said.

'I have only one dream: I want to finish the windmill before I retire next year,' said Boxer. Horses and pigs could retire at age twelve. 'Perhaps Benjamin will retire with me and I'll have a friend.'

Life was hard and the winter was long, icy and cold. There was very little food for all the animals, except for the pigs and dogs. Napoleon always had plenty of sugar on his own table. The other pigs could not eat sugar because it made them fat. Squealer was able to convince the animals that everything was much better now than with Mr Jones. Most of the animals didn't even remember what life was like with Mr Jones and they believed Squealer. All they knew was that they were usually hungry, cold and very tired. But Squealer convinced them that they were free now, and not slaves of Mr Jones. And that made all the difference!

Now there were many more mouths to feed as thirty-one young pigs were born. Napoleon educated them in the farmhouse kitchen, but planned to build a school for them. One day someone was cooking barley in the farmhouse kitchen and the smell was good. Napoleon announced that the barley was only for the pigs. It was used to make beer and the news went around that every pig received a big mug of beer daily.

In April, Animal Farm became a Republic and it was necessary to elect a President. There was only one candidate: Napoleon.

He was elected by all the animals. There were more parades and speeches by Squealer, and the animals were more tired and much hungrier now than during the days of Manor Farm — but they didn't remember.

ACTIVITIES

The text and *beyond*

Comprehension check

1 Choose the correct answer — a, b, c or d.

1 Who warned the animals of the attack on the farm?
   a ☐ The pigeons.
   b ☐ Moses.
   c ☐ Muriel.
   d ☐ No one.

2 Who noticed that Frederick's men were putting explosives around the windmill?
   a ☐ Squealer.
   b ☐ Napoleon.
   c ☐ Benjamin.
   d ☐ The pigeons.

3 What did the animals do when they saw the terrible black cloud of smoke?
   a ☐ They ran to hide in the barn.
   b ☐ They attacked the men bravely.
   c ☐ They went to look for Napoleon.
   d ☐ They ran to the big gate and escaped from the farm.

4 Why did Napoleon decide to grow barley in the garden?
   a ☐ Barley was an important brain food for the pigs.
   b ☐ Mr Whymper told him to grow the barley.
   c ☐ Napoleon wanted to sell the barley to the nearby farmers.
   d ☐ Barley was necessary to make alcoholic drinks like beer and whisky.

5 Who was elected President of the Republic of Animal Farm?
   a ☐ Squealer.
   b ☐ Napoleon.
   c ☐ Snowball.
   d ☐ Boxer.

ACTIVITIES

Characters

2 Write a description of the characters below. Use the words in the word basket. Some words can be used more than once.

> bad • bad tempered • brave • caring • clever • determined
> dishonest • enormous • fast talker • fat • friendly • good • hard worker
> honest • intelligent • jealous • kind • liar[1] • never complains
> obedient • old • selfish • sly • strong • stupid • tough
> uncaring • unfriendly • unkind • wise • young

Napoleon ....

Squealer ....

Snowball ....

Boxer ....

Benjamin ....

Clover ....

---

1. **liar**: a person who doesn't tell the truth; this person tells lies.

CHAPTER **10**

BOXER

When Boxer's hoof was better, he worked harder than ever. However, he became thinner and weaker. Clover and Benjamin told him to look after his health, but Boxer didn't listen. He wanted to finish the windmill before he retired. Late one summer evening two pigeons brought the terrible news: 'Boxer has fallen! He's at the windmill and he's lying on his side. He can't get up!'

About half the animals on the farm rushed up the hill. Poor Boxer couldn't move and some blood was coming out of his mouth. Clover was very upset and asked, 'Boxer, what happened?'

Boxer whispered, 'I can't breathe. But it doesn't matter. You'll be able to finish the windmill without me. I've brought lots of stones for the new wall. I think I should retire…'

'We need help, immediately!' cried Clover. 'Someone must go and call Squealer!'

BOXER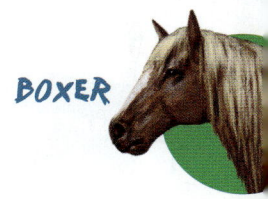

Squealer arrived and said, 'Comrade Napoleon and I are very sorry! Comrade Boxer, you are one of the best workers on the farm and Napoleon will send you to the Veterinary Hospital in Willingdon. You will have expert care! Don't worry!'

Boxer was taken back to his stall and he stayed there for two days. He wanted to get better so that he could retire and enjoy the grassy fields with Benjamin. And during his free time he could learn the remaining twenty-two letters of the alphabet. Boxer was alone in his stall when the lorry came to take him away. All the other animals were working in the fields when Benjamin galloped to them.

He was very upset and shouted, 'Quick! Come at once! They're taking Boxer away!'

The animals ran back to the barn and saw a lorry, pulled by two horses with words written on its side. An older man was sitting on the driver's seat.

'Good-bye, Boxer! Good-bye!' said the animals, happily.

'Fools! Fools!' cried Benjamin. 'Don't you see what's written on the side of that lorry?' The animals looked but couldn't read the words. Benjamin read, '*Alfred Simmonds, Horse Slaughterer*. Don't you understand? They are taking Boxer to the knacker's!'[1]

A loud cry of horror came from the animals.

'Boxer!' cried Clover, 'Get out! Get out quickly! They're taking you to your death.' All the animals cried, 'Get out, Boxer!' Poor Boxer was very weak and couldn't move.

Three days later Boxer died. Squealer hurried to give the news. 'Our Comrade Boxer died at the Veterinary Hospital.

---

1. **knacker** : a person who buys old horses and kills them for their meat, bones, leather.

CHAPTER 10

The veterinarians did everything to save his life. He had the best care, but Boxer was too old and weak. Napoleon paid for the most expensive medicines! I heard Boxer's last words: Long live Comrade Napoleon! Napoleon is always right'. Then he said, 'I've heard rumours that some animals think that Boxer was sent to the knacker's! What a terrible thought! The lorry you saw belonged to the knacker, but it was bought by the Veterinary Hospital. There was no time to change the name on the lorry. I am sure you all understand this!'

The seasons came and went, and the years passed. No one remembered the days before the rebellion, except Clover, Benjamin, Moses the raven and a few pigs. Squealer was so fat that he could hardly see out of his eyes. The new animals accepted everything they were told about the rebellion and the principles of Animalism. However, most of them didn't understand much.

The farm was well organized and quite successful. The windmill was complete, and the farm had new machinery. The harvest brought a lot of money, and the farm was richer now than in the past. However, the animals were not richer — except for the pigs and the dogs. Napoleon always said that true happiness was found in working hard and living in a very simple way.

Squealer continued giving his speeches about how everything was getting better and better. Most of the animals believed him. The pigs and the dogs got fatter, but the other animals were usually hungry and cold. The older animals couldn't remember what life was like before the rebellion, but Benjamin remembered clearly. He often said that hunger, suffering and disappointment were the law of life for the animals. And yet the animals never gave up hope. They were still the only farm in England that was owned by the animals!

BOXER

One day the animals had a shocking surprise: they saw Squealer walking on his hind[2] legs, and then they saw a long line of pigs all walking on their hind legs! To add to this surprise, they noticed that the Seven Commandments were not on the barn wall anymore. There was only one commandment that said:

ALL ANIMALS ARE EQUAL BUT SOME ANIMALS ARE MORE EQUAL THAN OTHERS.

The next day the pigs started to carry whips in their trotters when they supervised the work on the farm. Some pigs bought a radio and others were going to get a telephone. Napoleon began to wear Mr Jones's clothes and hat proudly, and smoked his pipe.

A week later, a number of carts drove up to the farm. Several farmers were invited to visit the farm and then met in the farmhouse with Napoleon and the other pigs. Clover and the other animals saw them arrive and they were very curious. Clover led the way to the farmhouse and some of the animals were tall enough to look inside the windows. The pigs were sitting comfortably in their chairs and playing a game of cards and cheating. Everyone was talking, arguing and drinking beer. No one noticed the curious animals outside the windows.

Then Mr Pilkington got up and spoke to the other farmers and the pigs. 'We farmers are pleased that we have become good friends. We can certainly do a lot of business together in the future. We have also learned that your lower animals do more work and receive less food — a brilliant idea! We are going to do the same thing on our farms: longer hours and less food! Please remember that you have your lower animals to deal with... but we, too, have our lower classes!'

---

2. **hind** : the back legs of an animal.

CHAPTER 10

He raised his beer mug and said, 'My toast [3] is to the success of Animal Farm!' Everyone at the big table laughed and cheered.

Napoleon got up with his beer mug in his trotter and said, 'We, too, are glad that we have become good neighbours. Some things have changed on this farm. The word Comrade is not used anymore, and the white hoof and horn that were on the green flag have been removed. And the name of the farm is no longer Animal Farm, but Manor Farm — the correct and original name. My toast is to the success of Manor Farm!' Everyone cheered.

The animals outside couldn't believe their eyes: there was no difference between the pigs and the men! The fat faces of the pigs were like the fat faces of the men; and the fat faces of the men were like the fat faces of the pigs. It was impossible to say which was which.

---

3. **toast** : (here) when you drink and wish a person or group of people success and good luck.

ACTIVITIES

The text and *beyond*

Comprehension check

1 Answer the following questions.

1. What bad news did the pigeons bring?
2. What did Boxer say to Clover?
3. Where did Squealer want to send Boxer?
4. What did Boxer want to do in his free time when he retired?
5. What did Benjamin tell the animals about the lorry?
6. How did Squealer change the story of the lorry?
7. What were Squealer's speeches like?
8. What was life at Animal Farm really like?
9. What was the only new commandment on the barn wall?
10. In what ways did the pigs change?
11. What did Clover and the other animals see through the windows of the farmhouse?
12. What difference was there between the pigs and the men?

T: GRADE 5

Speaking: recent personal experiences

2 Clover, Benjamin and Moses remembered many things about their past personal experiences. Clover lost her dear companion, Boxer. They all realized that life was much more difficult now than before. They were always hungry, tired and cold. Things were getting worse, not better. They were sad and very disappointed, because they couldn't trust their new "leaders". Talk with your partner about your personal experiences. Use these questions to help you.

1. Talk about a recent experience you have had.
2. What has this experience taught you?
3. Would you prefer to discuss a personal experience with a best friend or with a parent?
4. What was your happiest or best personal experience?
5. Do you think your past experiences will influence your behaviour in the future?

Crossword puzzle

3 Have fun with this crossword puzzle!

ACROSS

2 A place where there are big stones.
5 Something that is fake.
6 A substance that can harm or kill you if you eat it.
9 A grain used to make beer and whisky.
11 Very wild and dangerous.

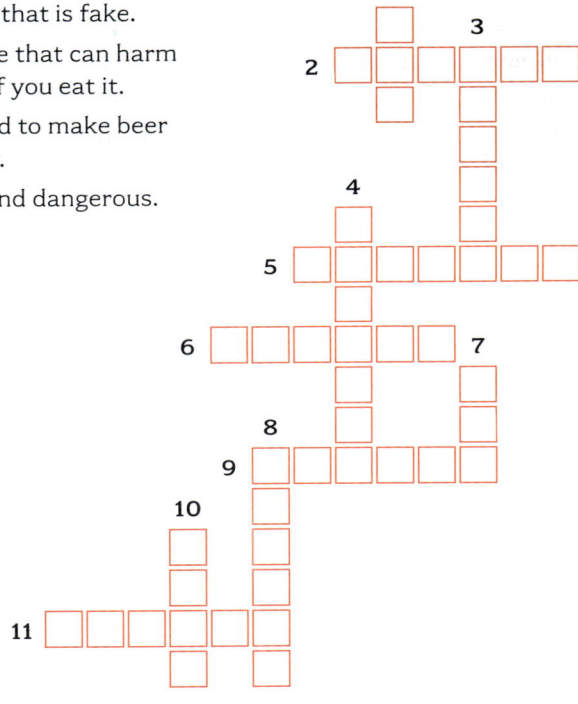

DOWN

1 A big glass of beer.
3 To stop working when you are old.
4 Adult male chicken.
7 Very clever; difficult to trust.
8 Small piece of metal fired from a gun.
10 The noise a dog makes.

Vladimir Lenin.

Animal Farm: An Allegory

What *is* Animal Farm?

Animal Farm is an allegory of the Russian Revolution (1917-1918). An allegory is a story where the characters and events are symbols of something else. George Orwell always criticized[1] dictatorships and totalitarian societies, and this is why he wrote *Animal Farm*, which is a strong criticism of Russian Communism.[2]

What was the Russian Revolution of 1917-1918 and what followed?

The Russian Revolution started in 1917 when the poor farmers and the working class revolted[3] against Tsar Nicholas II, the emperor. These people lived a difficult life of poverty and hunger. They were led by Vladimir Lenin and a group of revolutionaries called Bolsheviks.

---

1. **criticize** : disagree with something because you think it is wrong.
2. **communism** : a political belief that all people are equal, and that workers should control the means of producing things.
3. **revolt (verb)** : when people go against the political system of their country in a violent way.

A new communist government was created: the USSR (Union of the Soviet Socialist Republics).

After Lenin's death in 1924, Joseph Stalin and Leon Trotsky, both important members of the Communist party, disagreed as to the ideas and methods to follow. Trotsky was removed from the Communist party and was later thrown out of the country. In 1927 Stalin became the dictator of Russia. During his rule there was no room for criticism and all sources of information were strictly controlled. Stalin's secret police were feared by the people. Stalin died in 1953, three years after Orwell's death.

Themes that are presented

Orwell believed strongly in socialism,[4] but he felt that the Soviet Union achieved these ideals in a terribly cruel way. In *Animal Farm* he not only condemns dictators, but also their lies and hypocrisy.[5] The changes in the Seven Commandments and Squealer's lies and clever speeches are examples of this hypocrisy. At first all the animals were equal, but as time went on the class structure changed. Before a common enemy like Mr Jones, all the animals were together. But when the enemy was no longer present, things changed and separate classes were created. The pigs and the dogs were part of a different class from the other animals. At the end of the story, Mr Pilkington clearly talked about the lower classes.

The natural division between mental and physical work quickly appeared when Squealer talked about the pigs' brain work. He explained that brain workers were very important, because they made the right decisions for the other animals. Therefore, the pigs needed all

---

4. **socialism** : a set of left-wing political principles where everyone has an equal opportunity to benefit from a country's wealth, and the country's main industries are owned by the state.
5. **hypocrisy** : when you pretend to have qualities that you do not have; falsity.

Joseph Stalin.

kinds of special attention. The pigs' intelligence, however, was always used to their benefit and never to the benefit of the other animals. When Boxer said, 'Napoleon is always right' and 'I will work harder', we can see the comparison with Stalin's rule. During Stalin's time it was impossible to question authority or the ruling class; this could lead to oppression[6] and death.

Animal Farm clearly shows how power can bring corruption,[7] particularly when the power is in the hands of only one individual. This can be seen all through history with dictators, emperors, kings, queens and other rulers. At the end of the story the pigs were like the humans, with all their faults, habits and desires.

The characters

Orwell created animal characters that represented the people of the Russian Revolution and the USSR:

---

6. **oppression** : cruelty, hardship, injustice.
7. **corruption** : dishonesty, evil.

- **Mr Jones**, the farmer, represented **Tsar Nicolas II**, the last Russian emperor.
- **Old Major** represented **Vladimir Lenin**, the leader of the revolution.
- **Snowball** represented **Leon Trotsky**, the revolutionary leader.
- **Napoleon** represented **Joseph Stalin**, the dictator.
- **Squealer** represented **Vladimir Molotov**, Stalin's assistant and head of Communist propaganda.[8]
- The **fierce dogs** represented the **secret police**.
- **Boxer** represented the **farmers and workers** who believed in the system and didn't question authority.
- **Benjamin** represented the **free thinkers** who chose not to be involved in politics, because they realized that it was useless.

Comprehension check

1 Answer the following questions.

1. Why did Orwell write *Animal Farm*?
2. What was the Russian Revolution of 1917-1918?
3. Why were the changes in the Seven Commandments examples of hypocrisy and lies?
4. When did Joseph Stalin become dictator and how was his rule?
5. Why did the class structure change in *Animal Farm*?
6. How did the pigs use their intelligence?
7. How did power corrupt the pigs?

Class discussion

2 Work with a partner and present your answers to the class.

1. Give examples of cruel, corrupt dictators in history.
2. Give examples of cruel, corrupt dictators today.

---

8. **propaganda** : information that is often not accurate and used to influence people.

AFTER READING

What happened?

1 Read the sentences below and decide if they are true (T) or false (F). Correct the false ones.

		T	F
1	Napoleon taught the animals the song 'Beasts of England'.	☐	☐
2	The animals rebelled and broke down the door of the storage shed because they were very hungry.	☐	☐
3	Snowball wrote the Seven Commandments on the barn wall.	☐	☐
4	Milk and apples were considered brain foods for all the animals.	☐	☐
5	Napoleon and Snowball never agreed on anything, particularly on the windmill.	☐	☐
6	After Snowball's disappearance, Napoleon became the leader and began dealing with humans.	☐	☐
7	The windmill was destroyed twice.	☐	☐
8	Mr Frederick paid Napoleon for the pile of wood with a cheque.	☐	☐
9	The seasons passed and the animals were hungrier and colder than with Mr Jones.	☐	☐
10	The animals couldn't tell the difference between the pigs and the men who visited the farm at the end of the story.	☐	☐

Who said it?

2 Match the name of the character with the sentence.

> Benjamin   Snowball   Boxer   Napoleon
> Old Major   Mr Jones   Squealer

1 'Man's only interest is himself.' ....
2 'Get the whips! Stop those animals!' ....
3 'Donkeys live a long time.' ....
4 'Science has shown us that milk and apples are necessary food for us pigs.' ....
5 'A windmill is something wonderful!' ....
6 'Comrades, the windmill is nonsense! Don't vote for it!' ....
7 'I will work harder.' ....

AFTER READING

Who was it?
3 Match the name of the character with the sentences.

1. ☐ Mr Whymper
2. ☐ Boxer
3. ☐ Benjamin
4. ☐ Mollie
5. ☐ Clover
6. ☐ Moses
7. ☐ Squealer
8. ☐ Snowball
9. ☐ Napoleon
10. ☐ Muriel

a She liked wearing ribbons on her pretty head.
b He told the animals stupid stories about Sugarcandy Mountain.
c She was the mother of four foals.
d He was an unimportant lawyer and Napoleon's agent.
e He made drawings of the windmill.
f He liked drinking beer and whisky.
g She read the commandments on the barn wall to Clover.
h He was a big talker and convinced the animals.
i He wanted to finish the windmill before retiring.
j He read the sign on the lorry that took Boxer away.

What about you?
4 Answer the following questions.

1 Who was your favourite character and why?
....
2 What was your favourite part of the story?
....
3 Which character or characters did you dislike and why?
....
4 What did you learn from this story?
....
5 Can you relate or compare this story to another one you know?
....

This reader uses the expansive reading approach: where reading is not only the enjoyment of the story and the discovery of a new language, but an opportunity to make cultural connections.

The new language introduced in this step of our **Reading & Training** series is listed below and language from lower steps is included too. For a complete list for all six steps, see *The Black Cat Graded Readers Handbook* at *blackcat-cideb.com*.

Step TWO B1.1

Verb tenses

Present Perfect Simple: indefinite past with *yet*, *already*, *still*; recent past with *just*; past action leading to present situation

Past Perfect Simple: in reported speech

Verb forms and patterns

Regular verbs and most irregular verbs
Passive forms with *going to* and *will*
So / *neither* / *nor* + auxiliaries in short answers
Question tags (in verb tenses used so far)
Verb + object + full infinitive (e.g. *I want you to help*.)
Reported statements with *say* and *tell*

Modal verbs

Can't: logical necessity
Could: possibility
May: permission
Might (present and future reference): possibility; permission
Must: logical necessity
Don't have to / haven't got to: lack of obligation
Don't need to / needn't: lack of necessity

Types of clause

Time clauses introduced by *when*, *while*, *until*, *before*, *after*, *as soon as*
Clauses of purpose: *so that*; *(in order) to* (infinitive of purpose)

Step 2

If you enjoyed this reader, try another one in Step Two...

- *The Human Comedy*, by William Saroyan **(Life Skills)**
- *Murder on the Orient Express*, by Agatha Christie
- *Animal Tales*, by Rudyard Kipling et al.

Step 3

...or take a step forward to Step Three!

- *1984*, by George Orwell
- *Death on the Nile*, by Agatha Christie
- *The Time Machine*, by H.G. Wells